CREATE YOUR
special
wedding

CREATE YOUR

special
wedding

LUCINDA GANDERTON

Photographs by Lucy Mason

Styling by Malena Burgess

SOURCEBOOKS, INC.®
NAPERVILLE ILLINOIS

For Hannah Alice and Gracie Mary

Sourcebooks, Inc.
P.O. Box 4410, Naperville, Illinois 60567-4410
(630) 961-3900
FAX: (630) 961-2168

Editor: Alison Moss
Designer: Bet Ayer

Printed in Italy

MQ 10 9 8 7 6 5 4 3 2 1

ISBN: 1-57071-606-4

contents

Every wedding day is a unique expression of love, full of hope and promise for the future, and a special occasion to be shared with family and friends. Throughout the centuries, marriage has been celebrated by a combination of solemn ceremony and joyous festivity. In diverse cultures across the world, people join together in observing special rituals to bring good fortune to the newly married couple as they begin their life together.

The white wedding as we celebrate it today, however, is a relatively new tradition, although many of the attendant customs date back to early times. The concept developed in the mid-nineteenth century and became popular when Queen Victoria's daughters, clad in elegant satin crinolines and attended by a chorus of aristocratic bridesmaids, married their European dukes and princes. The trend for white gowns and veils gradually filtered down through society to become a lasting and established fashion.

At a time when clothing was sewn by hand, only the wealthiest could afford to purchase a special dress to be worn only once, so most brides wore their best outfits and bonnets. Blue was a favorite color, symbolizing loyalty and fidelity. The maxim, "married in blue, you'll always be true" is echoed today by girls who wear a hidden blue ribbon for luck. By contrast, American Republican women favored red dresses as a mark of defiance, and in Iceland, black velvet with metallic embroidery was customary. In 1861, the male guests were as colorful as the women. A fashion journal for that year advised them to wear "frock coats of blue, claret or mulberry color, trousers of pale drab or lavender doeskin and patterned waistcoats."

Other integral elements and symbols that make up today's wedding derive from ancient customs from many different countries. Rice is a symbol of fecundity in India, so handfuls of dry rice were thrown over the bride and groom at Hindu weddings. This became widespread, and nowadays throwing confetti (the name derives from the Italian term "little sweets") is an essential and enjoyable element of the event.

The tiered wedding cake is a relic of Roman weddings, where the couple ate a special cake made of salt, water, and flour. A flat, brittle cake was baked for a medieval English bride, and was broken over her head by female friends. The manner in which the pieces fell predicted the success of her marriage.

The lucky horseshoe, which some brides carry, is a crescent symbol of growth and good luck from the Far East; a ringing bell protects against evil, as well as being another fertility charm; while the heart is a universal symbol of love. The subtle, lace garter, worn by some brides, is a reminder of more riotous days, when a bride would tie a bunch of brightly colored ribbons around her knee and distribute

them among the groom's friends after the
ceremony!

However grand or informal your own wedding plans are, you
will undoubtedly wish to include some of these elements.
Although there are now countless etiquette guides, magazines,
books, and websites brimming with information, as well as specialist
wedding planners who can advise you on how to plan the perfect
day, you can easily tailor your wedding to your particular tastes.

This book, which features modern reworkings of popular traditions,
will help you personalize your wedding day and make it a memorable
event for the two of you and your guests. It is intended to be a
source of inspiration and a springboard for your own creativity.

Create Your Special Wedding is divided into five sections, which
progress from original designs for stationery items and flower
arrangements, through elegant accessories for the bride and her
attendants and items for the reception. It finishes with a chapter
featuring unique gifts to make for your marital home. The stylish
projects cover a range of basic craft skills, from working with paper
and flowers to sewing and beadwork. All of them are easily
achievable, and most of the equipment required will be on hand in
your house. Some projects can be completed in an afternoon by a
beginner, while others, such as the heirloom white quilt, are more of a
labor of love. Recruit your friends and get the whole family to share in
making the finishing touches that will complete your wedding.

stationery

Whether you are arranging a large wedding or an intimate ceremony with a few guests, meticulous planning is vital for the day to run smoothly. In addition to the official paperwork, you will find yourselves with growing piles of forms, receipts, and brochures, as well as letters and cards from friends and relations.

The projects in this chapter not only include stationery items such as invitations, order of service cards and thank you cards, but also decorative items you can make to help you store all your wedding papers, literature, and the inspirational pictures and sketches that you are using to build the look for the big day.

Try to be organized from the beginning. Start with an action list and, when the date and place have been decided, draw up a timetable so that nothing will be missed. Confirm all arrangements in writing and file copies of the letters. Make a contact list to keep important names and phone numbers on hand. Keep these all together in the organizer file on page 14, which has sections for filing copies of important letters along with pockets for storing scraps of material, trimmings, and other interesting bits and pieces.

Your most important list will be the guest list. Invitations should be issued at least six weeks in advance of the wedding to give people time to make any necessary arrangements. The time and care involved when you create you own invitations and cards will add a distinctive note to the event from the outset. Look for translucent and pearlized papers, lacy Japanese tissue and textured cards at specialist stationers and suppliers, and find colored envelopes to match.

There are many etiquette books that advise on the wording for the invitations, which can be as formal or informal as you wish. It is a good idea to include a map and a list of local hotels for those who will be traveling a long distance. Keep a note of all the acceptances and declinations as they come in, and store the cards in the pretty box on page 24.

The present list should not be sent with the invitations. As a matter of courtesy, you should only give it out when requested. To avoid any confusion once the gifts have been unwrapped, keep a checklist of the gifts as they arrive, noting who they are from. Express your thanks by making a thank you card with a personal, handwritten message for each giver.

Mr. and Mrs. Andrew Sibsall
request the pleasure of your company
at the marriage of their daughter
Sophia
to
Mr. Jack Thompson
at St. Paul's Church, London, W.1.
on Saturday 23rd August
at 3 o'clock
and afterwards at
Claridge's

R.S.V.P.
110 Eaton Square
London S.W.1

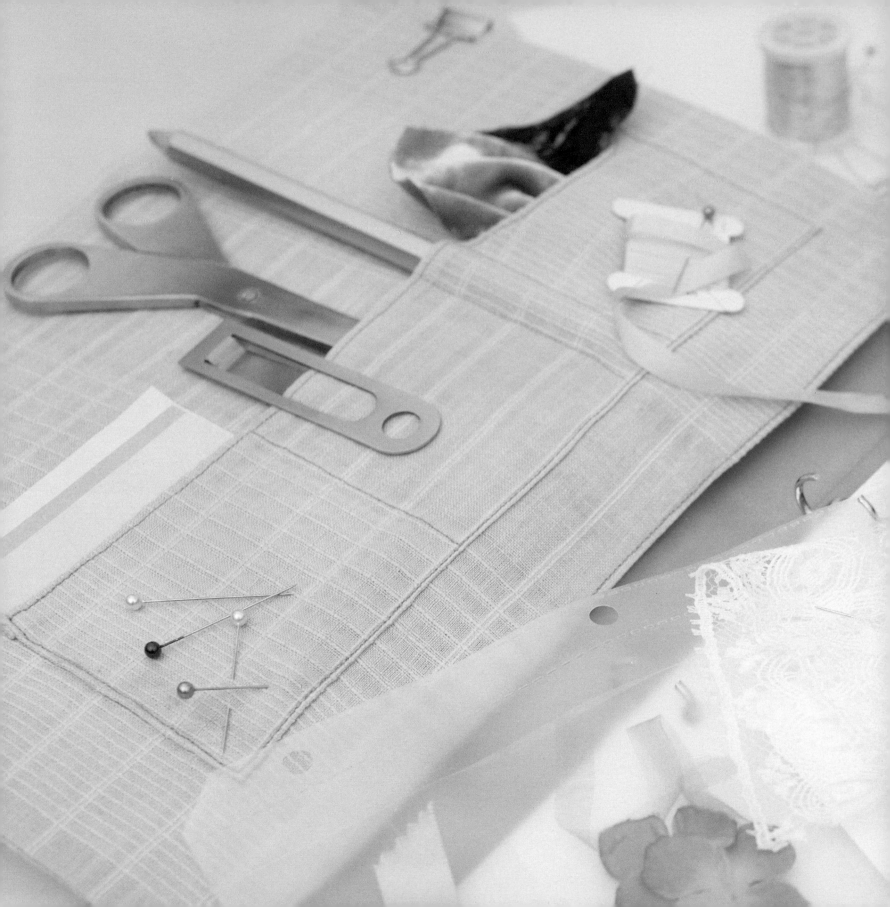

organizer file

As soon as the wedding date has been agreed upon, arrangements for the day begin to take shape and the serious planning gets underway. Be organized from the outset and keep track of all your ideas and useful contacts with a multipurpose file. Use it to build up a visual resource of your favorite images. Collect pictures torn from magazines, designer sketches, swatches of material, and samples of ribbon. There is space for leaflets and brochures from bridal stores, caterers, and florists to be filed alongside official forms and letters, so that all your reference material is held safely in one place.

stationery

15

A plain ring binder can be easily dressed up with a practical linen cover, complete with a useful pocket to hold pens, a ruler, and stationery. As well as the usual dividers and indexing leaves, look for divided transparent file sheets, which can be used to store pieces of fabric, buttons, trimmings, business cards, and other small items.

MATERIALS
Plastic ring binder
15 x 45in./40 x 115cm colored linen
Matching sewing thread
File inserts
Tape measure
Dressmaker's scissors
Sewing machine
Sewing kit
Iron

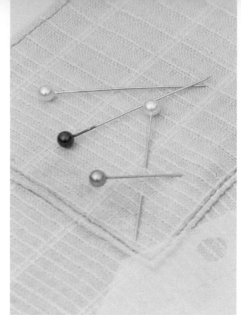

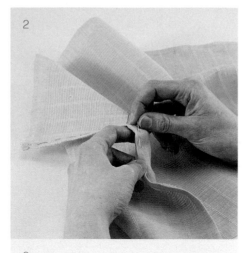

1 Open the ring binder and measure the height and full width. Cut a long rectangle of fabric 1in./3cm deeper than the binder and twice the width.

2 Press and tack a ⅓in./1cm double hem at each short end of the fabric, thread the sewing machine with the matching thread, and machine stitch ⅛in./3mm from the outside edge. Remove the tacking thread.

3 Enlarge the pocket template on page 118 on a photocopier and use it to cut a piece of fabric with a ⅓in./1cm seam allowance. Turn under the allowance, then pin and tack in place. Clip the seam allowance along the curve, if necessary, to give a smooth line.

4 Machine stitch along what will become the open side of the pocket ⅛in./3mm from the edge. Remove the tacking thread and press.

5 With the rectangle of fabric right side up, pin the pocket to one short end, 1½in./4cm in from the hem. Tack it in place.

6 Machine stitch along the side and bottom edges, then work three parallel rows of stitches, using the markings on the template as a guide, to create three separate pockets.

7 Remove the tacking. Fold the cover in half widthways and clip a small notch at the center point of each long edge.

8 With the rectangle of fabric right side up, place the open ring binder over the cover so that the notches line up to the center of the spine and fold the cover around the sides. Pin the two edges of fabric together at the top and bottom of the binder, leaving a ½in./1.5cm allowance.

9 Remove the binder, tack, and then machine stitch right across the top and bottom of the cover. Remove the tacking thread. Clip the corners and turn the cover right side out. Press well.

10 Slip the ring binder back inside the fabric cover, making sure that the seam allowance lies flat behind the spine.

11 Clip your own indexer or dividers and transparent pocket pages into the file.

12 The pocket can hold fabric and ribbon swatches, as well as stationery items.

flowers

confetti box

Throwing paper confetti, rice, or fresh flower petals over the newly married couple is a favorite ritual for all the guests to enjoy after the solemnity of a marriage service. You can make these confetti boxes to be filled and distributed among your guests on the day, or you may wish to make the wedding preparations truly interactive.

Complete the box as far as step 5 and send it out with the invitation cards as part of a "do-it-yourself" kit. Include two lengths of piping cord for the handles and a photocopy of the folding guide on page 20, and ask your guests to make up their own boxes. All they will have to do is provide the confetti!

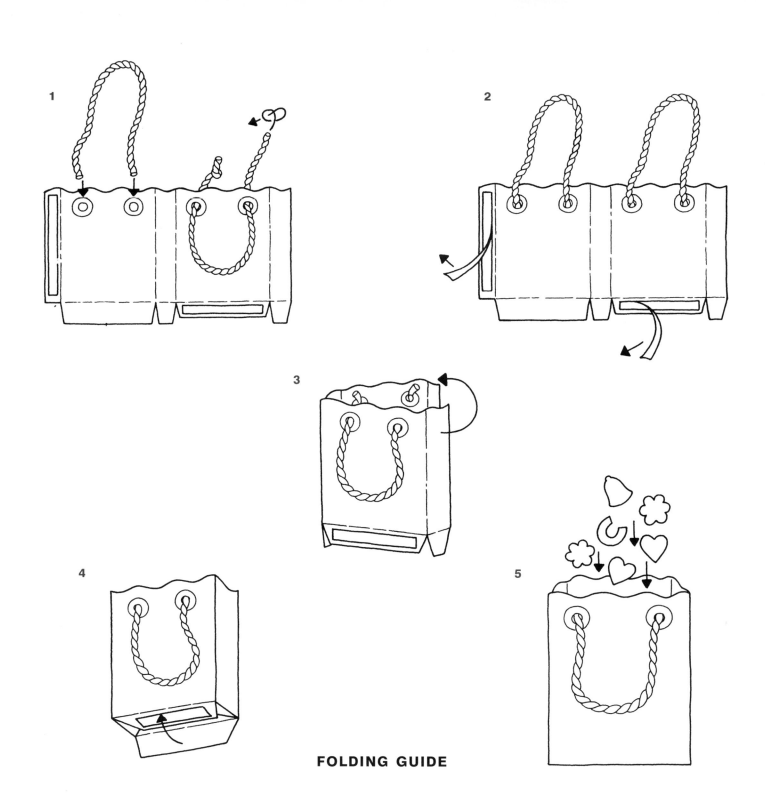

FOLDING GUIDE

The box is made from white card with a slightly ridged surface. Use the same card for the invitation on page 22 to give the two items a complementary feel. If the confetti boxes are going to be given out on the wedding day, you could write names on the front or add a tie-on label for each guest.

MATERIALS

Tracing paper
Thin card
Textured white card
½in./1.5cm eyelets and eyelet tool
Cotton piping cord
Double-sided tape
Sharp pencil
Metal ruler
Craft knife
Cutting mat
Small scissors
Decorative scissors

1 Enlarge the template on page 119 on a photocopier and trace it onto the thin card. Carefully cut along the outline using the craft knife and metal ruler on a cutting mat, then cut out the four holes with small scissors. Place the card template onto the textured white card and draw around it with a sharp pencil. Cut out with scissors.

2 Lay the textured card right side up on the cutting mat. Following the template on page 119, carefully score the card with the craft knife and ruler where indicated by the dotted lines.

3 Cut out the four holes with scissors. Following the manufacturer's instructions, fasten a metal eyelet into each one.

4 Cut a wavy line along the top edge of the box with decorative craft scissors.

5 Using the template on page 119 as a guide, fix double-sided tape to the two shaded areas.

6 Cut two 12in./30cm lengths of piping cord for the handles. Thread the two ends of the first piece through the eyelets from the right side and tie a secure knot in each end. Repeat for the second handle.

7 Fold up the box along the scored lines. Peel the backing off the tape. Stick the narrow side flap to the back of the wide side flap. Fold up the short bottom flaps and press the wide bottom flap against the narrow bottom flap.

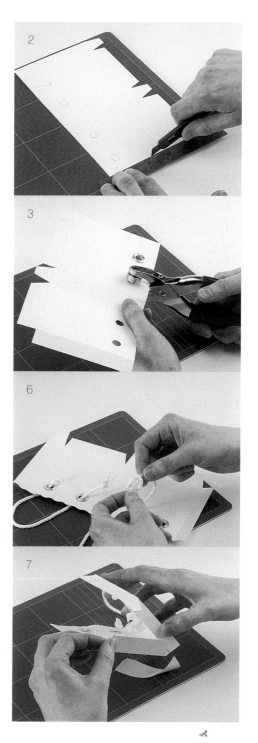

stationery

invitation

Confetti shapes are trapped and stitched down under a delicate layer of transparent organza to make this distinctive card. The formal wording of the invitation, with details of the date, time, and location, can either be written by hand in your best calligraphy, or printed on a separate sheet of paper to fix inside the card. You can make a matching acceptance card from a 3in./8cm square of textured card with a single piece of confetti glued in the center and wording on the back.

MATERIALS
Textured white card
Paper confetti
Pale pink organza
Matching sewing thread
Metal ruler and sharp pencil
Cutting mat
Craft knife
Glue stick
Eraser
Craft scissors
Embroidery scissors
Sewing machine

1 Cut a 5 x 8in./12 x 20cm rectangle of card. Mark the center of each long edge and rule a pencil line between the two points. On a cutting mat, score gently across this line using the craft knife and ruler.

2 Gently fold the card in half along the scored line.

3 Measure and lightly mark a 1½in./4cm square on the front of the card with a pencil and ruler, 1¼in./3cm down from the top edge and each side.

4 Using a small amount of adhesive, glue four pieces of confetti within the square. Carefully erase all the pencil marks.

5 Cut out a 2½in./6cm square of organza along the grain of the fabric. Make a ⅓in./8mm deep fringe around all four sides by pulling away a few threads along each edge.

6 Glue the organza square over the confetti shapes.

7 Open the card, thread the sewing machine with pink thread, and set the stitch length to medium. Stitch around the solid edge of the organza. Finish off the threads neatly on the wrong side.

8 Glue the handwritten or printed sheet with the details of the wedding to the inside of the card. Make sure that the glue is dry before placing inside an envelope.

acceptance cards box

Soon after the invitations have been mailed, your guests will begin to send back their replies. To keep track of numbers, you should mark off the names of the people who will be attending, and of those who are unable to come, on your guest list right away. Store the acceptance cards, letters, and any special notes you receive in this flower-edged box.

MATERIALS

Wire-framed scrim box
Blue and cream silk hydrangeas
Small pearl beads
Bunch of cake decorator's stamens
1in./2.5cm cream satin ribbon
Matching sewing thread
Craft scissors
Embroidery scissors
Tape measure
Sewing kit

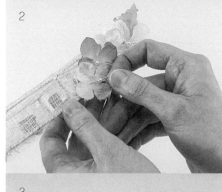

1 Snip off the individual silk flowers from the hydrangea heads with craft scissors and remove the plastic centers. Cut the large fabric leaves down into smaller leaf shapes, using the embroidery scissors to give a serrated edge.

2 Hand stitch the leaves and flowers along the outside rim of the box lid, leaving a 1in./2.5cm gap at the center of each side. Sew a pearl bead in the middle of each flower.

3 Take three stamens and fold them in half. Twist the folded ends together to form a small bunch, then slip it behind a silk flower. Sew securely to the box rim, making sure that the stitches are concealed by the flowers. Repeat at intervals around the lid.

4 Measure across the top and two side edges of the box lid and add 1¼in./4cm. Cut two lengths of ribbon to this measurement and hand stitch them across the lid to cover the wire struts. Make a narrow turning at each end of the ribbon and slip stitch in place on the inside rim.

5 Cover the wire struts of the box in the same way.

This parchment folder opens to reveal the order of service, which can be hand-written or printed on the inner leaf. A basic knowledge of crochet is needed to create the silver rings, but metal eyelets would look equally attractive. You could also make your own tassels following the method outlined on page 111.

MATERIALS

2 reels of silver machine embroidery thread
½in./12mm plastic rings
Marble effect heavy tracing paper
Parchment effect card
Small silver tassels
Size 2.5 crochet hook
Sharp pencil
Metal ruler
Craft scissors
Cutting mat
Craft knife
Hole punch
Glue stick

1 Make two silver rings. Holding the ends of both reels of silver thread and a plastic ring in one hand, and the crochet hook in the other, draw the thread through the center of the ring to make the working loop. Pull the thread through the loop, above the ring, to anchor it in place.

2 Work a round of half-treble stitches: * (thread over hook, draw the thread through the ring {3 loops on hook}, then draw the thread through all 3 loops). Repeat from * to cover the ring, then finish off with a slip stitch through the top of the first half-treble. Darn the loose ends into the wrong side and trim.

3 Cut a 3½ x 5½in./9 x 14cm rectangle of the heavy tracing paper to make a slip sheet to go inside the folded cover.

4 Cut a 6 x 8in./15 x 20cm rectangle from the parchment card. On the cutting mat, lightly score a line 2in./5cm from each short edge using the craft knife and metal ruler. Fold along the scored lines.

5 Punch a ¼in./6mm hole halfway down the edge of each short side. Glue the silver rings over the holes. Place the slip sheet inside and push the tassel loop through both rings. Pass the tassel through the loop to close the folder.

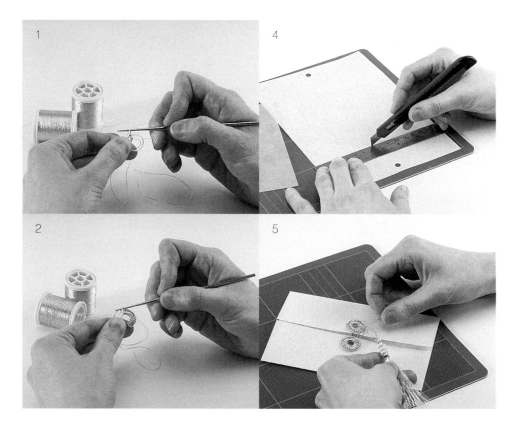

order of service

thank you card

Wedding presents should be acknowledged with a hand-written note. This personal thank you card incorporates a scaled-down print of your favorite wedding photograph. Make copies of the contact sheets or reduce an image on a photocopier or scanner.

MATERIALS

Marble-effect thin card
Japanese tissue paper
Copies of a 1½in./4cm
square photograph
Pearlized card
Sharp pencil
Metal ruler
Cutting mat
Craft knife
Glue stick
Craft scissors
Double-sided tape

1 Cut one 4in./10cm square and one 3¼in./8cm square from the thin marble-effect card.

2 Take the smaller square and mark a 1¼in./3cm square opening in the center. Cut out on a cutting mat using the craft knife and metal ruler.

3 Cut a 6in./15cm square of Japanese tissue paper. Glue the small square in the center of the tissue paper with a light coat of adhesive.

4 Make two diagonal cuts across the central square of tissue paper and cut off the outer corners. Fold the surplus tissue to the back of the card and glue down.

5 Glue the photograph to the wrong side of the tissue-covered frame, then stick the frame to the center of the large square of marble-effect card.

6 Cut a 9½ x 4¾in./24 x 12cm rectangle from the pearlized card. Mark a point 4¾in./12cm along each long edge and place right side up on the cutting mat. Score lightly between the two marks using the metal ruler and craft knife, then fold in half along the scored line. Stick the framed picture to the front of the card with double-sided tape, leaving an equal margin all round.

Flowers will be a vital decorative feature on your wedding day, creating the atmosphere with their inimitable color, perfume, and romance. The one essential accessory for every bride, whatever her outfit, is a bouquet, and she may even choose to wear fresh flowers in her hair. The groom, along with his groomsmen, will undoubtedly sport a boutonniere. Bridesmaids and flower girls will carry posies or baskets of petals, and corsages should be made up for the proud mothers. The floral theme can be carried through from the marriage ceremony to decorate the home or place where the reception is being held.

If either of you are gardeners, it is a great luxury to be able to use flowers you have grown yourselves; otherwise it is worth talking to your florist to find out which flowers will be available at the time of your wedding. Although many exotic species are imported from around the world and roses can be bought in the depths of winter, there is a certain charm in using flowers to match the season. Tender spring flowers—lilies-of-the-valley, forget-me-nots, and hyacinths—come in pastel shades and have an ethereal scent compared with the heady aroma of the full-blown roses, gerberas, and cornflowers of summer. An autumn wedding could feature heathers and golden leaves, while dark evergreens and red berries provide the keynotes for a winter wedding.

For the sentimental, the Language of Flowers, which attributes a specific symbolism to every plant, may help you to decide the flowers and foliage to use. Its origins lie in ancient history, and its vocabulary was first formalized in Persia, where specially chosen posies were used to convey clandestine messages. The Language spread to European courts in the 1700s, and by the nineteenth century, dictionaries of coded meanings were being published on both sides of the Atlantic.

Pink roses represent "happy love"; white roses suggest "worthy of love"; while a red rosebud's message is "pure and lovely." Rosemary, meaning "remembrance," was incorporated into the bouquets of Victorian brides, as was myrtle, which stands simply for "love." Honeysuckle and ivy aptly symbolize "bonds of friendship" and "wedded love" respectively, but be wary of camellia japonica, which means "my heart bleeds for you," or scabious, which stands for "unfortunate attachment."

bride's
bouquet

The large formal bouquets of previous generations, when the flowers were wired and twisted into tumbling cascades, have largely given way to the more natural and unstructured look of hand-tied bunches. These look especially dramatic when made up of just one type of bloom or a combination of different flowers in varying tones of one color.

For this romantic bouquet, a dome of the palest apricot roses has been circled with freesias, which have been chosen for their rich perfume as well as their cream petals. The glossy heart-shaped leaves create a dark background to emphasize the silhouette of the flowers. The rose stems have had their thorns removed and are simply bound with florist's tape, concealed by a generous length of wide translucent ribbon.

Ideally, the bouquet should be put together early on the morning of the wedding so that the flowers are at their best. If it has to be left in water to keep it fresh prior to the ceremony, make sure that the florist's tape does not become damp. The stems should be completely dry before the ribbon is tied around them and the bouquet is passed to the bride. Use a hairdryer if necessary to avoid any drips.

MATERIALS

10 roses
2 bunches of freesias
4 large leaves
1½yd/1.5m wide gauzy ribbon
Gardening gloves
Paper towel
Green florist's tape
Garden scissors
Tape measure

1 Wearing gardening gloves, carefully remove the thorns from the rose stems and strip off the leaves. Dry off all the stems with paper towel.

2 Group the roses into a domed bunch, holding the stems together in one hand.

3 Add the freesias around the edge, ensuring that the flowers all face outward.

4 Keeping the flowers in one hand, add the leaves, spacing them evenly around the edge of the bouquet.

5 Bind the stems securely with the florist's tape, from two-thirds of the way up the stems to just below the leaves.

6 Trim the stems so that they are all the same length.

7 Leaving about 18in./45cm free at one end, wrap the gauzy ribbon around the florist's tape to conceal it until 12in./30cm from the other end. Tie the ribbon ends into a beautiful bow to finish.

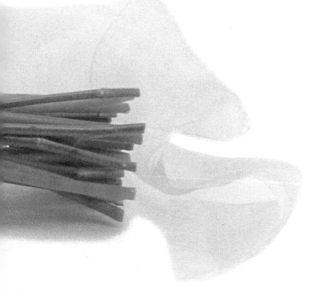

boutonniere

A classic single rose is a popular choice for making a boutonniere. Ideally, the bloom should be half open, not a tight bud, and shades of white, cream, or pale yellow will show up best against a dark formal jacket. Here, the unusual green tinge of the petals has been complemented with a large variegated ivy leaf.

The personalized tags used here are made from textured paper finished off with a small eyelet, but you could buy small tie-on labels from a specialist stationer's. Arrange the boutonnieres in a shallow box, lined with tissue paper to be distributed among the guests as they arrive for the ceremony; this task could be delegated to the bridesmaids or groomsmen. As a thoughtful touch, provide decorative pearl-headed pins to fasten the flowers in place.

MATERIALS
Cream roses
Large ivy leaves
Narrow ribbon
Small tie-on labels
Gardening gloves
Green florist's tape
Rose wire and wire cutters
Fine black pen
Tape measure
Scissors

1 Trim the stem of the rose to approximately 3in./8cm long and, wearing gardening gloves to protect your fingers, remove any thorns.

2 Bind the stems of the rose and ivy leaf together with rose wire. Twist the two ends of the wire together and trim with wire cutters. Carefully flatten the ends of the wire against the stems.

3 Cover the stems with florist's tape, winding it upward from the bottom of the stems, then downward. Make sure that the cut end of the stems are covered completely so that they don't bleed.

4 Write the name or initials of one of the guests onto a tie-on. Cut a 12in./30cm length of narrow ribbon and thread on the tag. Make a knot in the ribbon a short distance from the tag.

5 Tie the ribbon in a bow around the boutonniere.

flowers

bridesmaid's flower ball

The best silk flowers are now so sophisticated that they are indistinguishable from the real thing, and with a little imagination you can use them to create your own fantasy blooms in a kaleidoscope of colors.

At least twenty different types of flower have gone into this sumptuous flower ball, in shades that range through cream and bright yellow, dusty pink, and dark blue. Some of the original sprays were dismantled and the flower heads pinned directly to the polystyrene foundation; other flower heads were taken apart and the different colored petals and leaves were combined to make new and exotic flowers.

One word of warning: the flower ball should not be given to very young children, because inquisitive fingers could get hurt if the pins are removed.

The flower ball is designed to be carried by the younger bridesmaids in place of a traditional posy, but you could easily extend the idea to make pew ends for the church, or wall and table decorations for the reception. Polystyrene molds are available in various sizes and shapes, including cones, hearts, rings, and stars, which could all be covered with beautiful coordinating flowers.

MATERIALS
Selection of silk flowers
4in./10cm diameter polystyrene ball
Small glass beads
20in./50cm gauze ribbon
Craft scissors
Dressmaker's pins
Tape measure
Sewing kit

1 Carefully separate the individual silk flowers from their stalks, snipping them off with scissors if necessary.

2 Pin the largest flowers onto the polystyrene ball, spacing them evenly. Thread a small bead onto the pin first and press into the center of the flower to hold it securely in place.

3 To make the multicolored flowers, layer three or four different colored heads together, with the largest on the bottom.

4 Continue pinning single and layered flowers to the polystyrene, making sure that the colors are spread evenly across the surface of the ball.

5 Add individual green leaves to fill in any spaces that are left.

6 Cut a 12in./30cm length of ribbon and fold it into a loop to make the handle. Stitch the two ends together with a row of running stitch and draw up the thread. Stitch the gathered end to secure, then fix it into the ball, using several pins to make it secure.

7 Cut the ends of the remaining ribbon into fish tails. Fold the ribbon in half and gather the fold with running stitch as before. Pin the gathered end to the polystyrene ball, directly opposite the handle at the bottom of the ball.

floral urn

This spring flower group was inspired by the opulent still life paintings of the seventeenth-century Dutch masters. They delighted in painting an eclectic mix of flowers and foliage, massed into dense arrangements which tumbled from urns and vases.

Recreating their lush informality is not difficult. Choose seasonal flowers in your favorite colors, looking out for contrasting textures and forms. The heavy-petalled peonies, used here, complement the multiflowered hydrangea heads, whose shape is echoed by the more delicate guelder roses. Remember that the foliage should be as varied as the flowers. Dark-leaved box sprays, feathery wax flowers, and euphorbia all bring their distinctive characteristics to the arrangement.

The small-scale Versailles urn used for this project provides the height necessary for a trailing arrangement. To achieve a similar look with your own selection of flowers, create the main outline with foliage, use bold flowers to work up the central mass, and then add further greenery to soften the edges of the overall shape.

MATERIALS

Urn or similar container
Block of florist's foam
Green foliage including wax flower, berberis, euphorbia, and box
Peonies
Hydrangeas
Guelder roses
Polythene
Knife
Garden scissors

1 Make sure that the container you have chosen is watertight. Line it with polythene if necessary.

2 Trim the florist's foam to shape and fit it inside the container. Cover it with water and leave for one hour. Top up the level if the foam has soaked up all the water.

3 Cut seven or eight lengths of foliage in different shades of green. Strip the leaves 4in./10cm from the bottom of each length, then push them into the oasis to make a loose diamond shape.

4 Add the peonies to the bottom right of the arrangement, allowing them to fall forward naturally.

5 Fill in the left side of the arrangement with guelder rose heads so that the silhouette is roughly symmetrical. Add two or three guelder roses to the right side to balance the colors.

6 Add three blue hydrangea heads, fitting them in between the other large flower heads. This will complete the central mass of the group.

7 Cut several shorter lengths of greenery and use them to extend the lower edge of the arrangement so that they trail down on either side.

8 Fill in any spaces in the outline with light-colored flower sprays, such as euphorbia.

9 Complete the arrangement with two or three dark sprays of foliage hanging over the front of the urn in the center.

10 Time constraints may mean that your flower arrangement has to be made up some time before the reception takes place. If necessary, store it in a cool place overnight, and freshen it up the next morning by spraying with a fine mist of water.

centerpiece

This layered confection of frosted fruit is a delectable alternative to the standard flower arrangement. It would make an eye-catching display for the top table or a focal point for a buffet or drinks table.

Crystallized peaches, nectarines, and strawberries, in rich shades of pink and red, are arranged in tiers, and interspersed with leaves, bright orange kumquats, and the papery textures of physalis and lychees.

The antique cake stand lends a period feel to the centerpiece. Similar pressed-glass stands can be found in junk shops and second-hand stores, or ask members of the family to check if there is one stored away in a cupboard.

Make sure that all the fruit is dry before you start crystallizing it, and that it is fresh but not over ripe. Discard any pieces that are bruised or have any damage to the flesh. Once it has been crystallized, the fruit should be left in a cool place overnight, or until the egg white and sugar have hardened into a solid coating.

MATERIALS
2 eggs
Bag of castor sugar
Glass cake stand
Small pudding bowl
Selection of fruit including nectarines, peaches, strawberries, lychees, kumquats, and physalis
Sprays of green leaves
Mixing bowl
Egg whisk
Coarse sieve
Shallow dish
Pastry brush
Metal cooling rack
Scissors

1 Separate the eggs. Place the two whites in a mixing bowl and beat them gently with the whisk until they are well mixed but not stiff. Sift the castor sugar into a shallow bowl.

2 Using the pastry brush, coat a nectarine lightly with the liquid egg white. Holding it with the tips of your fingers, gently roll the fruit in the castor sugar until it is covered completely, then place on a metal cooling rack. Repeat this process to frost the rest of the nectarines, the peaches, and the strawberries. Arrange them in rows on the rack, making sure that they do not touch each other. Sprinkle a little more sugar over any patchy areas and leave to dry.

3 Place the small pudding bowl upside down in the center of the cake stand. This will provide the necessary support for the growing arrangement.

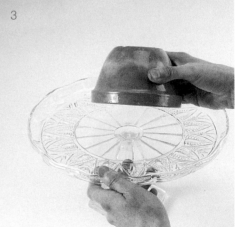

4 Shake each fruit gently to remove any excess sugar. Arrange the nectarines and peaches in a circle around the pudding bowl. Make a second tier of large fruit, fitting them carefully in the spaces between the first layer to keep the arrangement stable.

5 Make a small circle of strawberries on top of the nectarines and peaches, placing them so that the pointed ends face outwards.

6 Finish off the pyramid with a small cluster of lychees.

7 Place more lychees around the edge of the cake stand in between the peaches and the nectarines.

8 Tuck the kumquats into any spaces above the lychees.

9 Peel back the papery casing from the physalis to reveal the round berries inside. Place these in the spaces between the fruit in the second and third tiers.

10 Cut the foliage into single leaves and small sprays.

11 Tuck these in between the fruit, spacing them regularly across the whole arrangement.

garland

Delicate wild flowers, such as poppies and the sweetly named "love-in-a-mist," are not always easy to find and do not survive for long once they have been picked. Their naturalistic silk counterparts, however, are long lasting and can withstand being bent, wired, glued, and twisted to make this country-style circlet of flowers. The garland can be hung from the front door, on the wall of the reception room, or laid flat as a table decoration.

MATERIALS

Selection of silk grasses and flowers including wheat, blue poppies, delphinium, nigella "love-in-a-mist," and eucalyptus
Rose wire
Wire cutters
Flat-nosed pliers
Craft scissors
Glue gun

1 Gently bend two large wheat stalks into semicircles and bind them together with rose wire to form a circle. Use the pliers to twist the wire firmly and trim the ends with the wire cutters.

2 Cut the foliage into individual sprays and attach them to the foundation with short lengths of wire, spacing them evenly around the circle.

3 Divide the smaller flowers into sprays and attach them in the same way, filling in the gaps and covering any exposed wire.

4 Cut the heads from the poppy, delphinium, and nigella stems. Fix them in place on the garland at regular intervals using a hot glue gun. Finish off with the remaining leaves, adding them to the garland to fill in any spaces.

accessories

Every well-dressed woman knows that the right accessories can transform even the simplest outfit into a stylish ensemble, so it follows that the items the bride wears with her wedding gown, from headpiece to shoes, should be selected with the utmost care. The accessories that you make yourself, however, will make your outfit feel even more special.

Search your favorite craft and department stores, as well as specialist bridal shops, for fabrics and materials that will complement the dresses of yourself and your attendants. Look out for interesting beads and trimmings, luxurious velvets, fine cotton voiles, and metallic organzas. Most brides choose white or cream tones for their outfit, so a decorative bridal wrap, bag, or comb will add highlights of color and pattern to a predominantly neutral palette.

However modern your style, you may still want to abide by the old custom of wearing "something old, something new, something borrowed, something blue." This charming superstition links your past life with your family to your future life with your husband, with the color blue signifying fidelity. You may have inherited an heirloom lace veil that has been passed down through the generations, or you could slip your grandmother's embroidered handkerchief into your bag, as your "something old." Your dress and shoes will no doubt be "new," and you can "borrow" that desirable piece of jewelry you have always coveted from a friend, aunt, or sister, just for the day. Sew a tiny blue bow inside your hem to bring you luck or tie a blue ribbon around your bouquet.

The bridal veil is the one accessory that epitomizes the romance of a wedding. It is worn as a symbol of modesty and originated in the mid-nineteenth century when the white wedding first became fashionable. The earliest veils were made from sheer cotton or, for the very wealthy, the finest handmade lace. Once textile manufacture was mechanized, wide squares of decorated net became affordable and the new tradition was established.

Depending on the dress, today's bride can choose to wear a veil that reaches to her shoulders, waist, knees, or ankles. It can be held in place with a garland of fresh or silk flowers, a tiara, coronet, or Juliet cap, or you could make your own comb adorned with beaded flowers.

beaded comb

Glass-bead flowers, like these fragile-looking bloom and fern sprays, were first recorded as far back as the fifteenth century, when full scale bunches and posies were fashioned from wire and tiny rocaille beads on the Venetian glass-making island of Murano.

Making a whole bouquet may seem a daunting task today, but a few flowers in pale crystal shades make the perfect decoration for combs, clips, and other hair ornaments for both the bride and her attendants. Despite their delicate appearance, the finished flowers and sprays are quite robust, and can easily withstand being manipulated into the most ambitious hairstyle.

The bead petals and leaves are not difficult to make. Once you have mastered the technique for completing the basic wired shape, you can go on to devise ever more intricate flowers in myriad colors.

MATERIALS

Rose wire
1/10in./2mm rocaille beads
in pale green, apricot, fuchsia,
and clear glass
1/16in./1.5mm purple glass beads
Clear plastic comb
White felt
Wire cutters
Flat-nosed pliers
Scissors
PVA (white) glue
Ruler

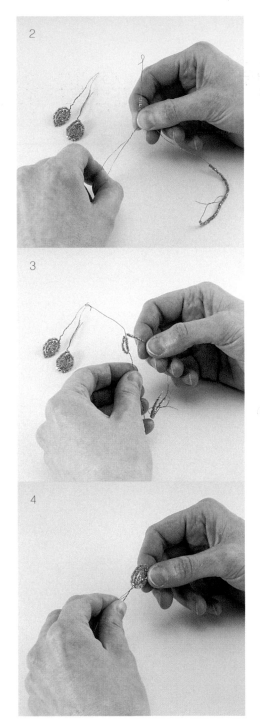

1 The three large flowers are each made up of five petals. For each petal, thread 46 beads onto a 12in./30cm length of wire.

2 Slide the first 6 beads along to 4in./10cm from the end. These will form the center of the petal. Bend the next 6in./15cm of wire into a loop and twist it to make the stalk.

3 Count off the next 8 beads. Take the wire up to the left and wrap it once around the center just above the top bead. Bring the wire down to the right and count off another 8 beads.

4 Wrap the wire once around the stalk just below the bottom bead. Make another round in the same way, with 12 beads on each side.

5 To finish off the petal, bend the center wire back behind the beads, then twist all four strands together.

6 Make four more in the same color. Hold them in a flower shape and twist the wire stalks firmly together using the pliers. Bend the petals gently into position.

7 Thread 3 beads in a different color onto a short length of wire and twist into a loop. Slip the ends of the wire between the petals, so that the beads lie in the center of the flower, and wrap them around the stalk. Make three flowers in apricot, fuchsia, and clear in this way.

8 The four leaf sprays are made from pale green beads. Thread 11 beads onto a 12in./30cm length of wire and slide them into the center. Pass one end of the wire through the first two beads and draw up into a loop.

9 Thread 13 beads onto one end of the wire, pass the end back through the first two beads and draw up. Make a similar loop on the other wire.

10 Thread both wires through three more beads to make a stalk. Make another two pairs of leaves, separated by a 4-bead stalk and finish off with a 5-bead stalk.

11 The three violets are made from the purple glass beads. Thread 18 beads onto an 8in./20cm length of wire and twist into a loop 1½in./4cm from one end to form a petal. Thread another 18 beads onto the long end, slide them to ⅛in./2mm from the first petal and twist into another 1½in./4cm loop.

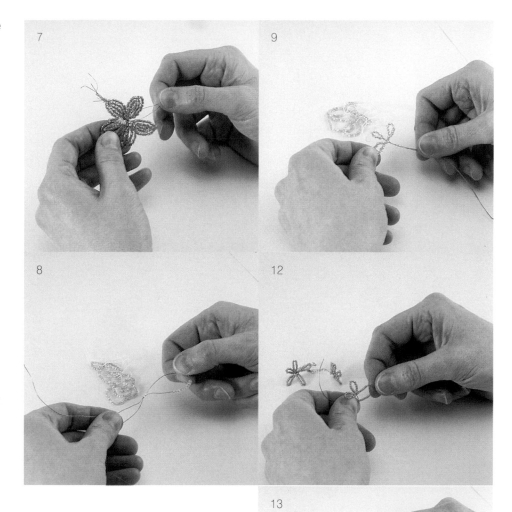

12 Make another three petals in the same way, then thread on one of the rocaille beads. Pass the wire into the center of the flower behind the petals, then thread both wires through 6 green glass beads to make a stalk.

13 Hold two leaf sprays at one corner of the comb so that the stems lie along the front top edge. Cut a 6in./15cm length of wire and bind it tightly over the stems and

in between the teeth to hold the sprays in place. Fix the other two sprays to the oppostie corner. Add a flower at each end in the same way, then fix the violets to the center. Attach the third flower to fill the remaining space.

14 Flatten any sharp ends with the pliers. Cut a strip of felt to fit along the back top edge of the comb and glue it in place to cover the wire completely.

Let your creative talents run wild with these exuberant pins, which can be worn in place of a brooch, to hold a scarf in position, or to adorn a hat.

They are made from bright feathers and beads threaded onto specially made wire shafts (available from good bead and jewelry suppliers). Look out for large beads in unusual shapes. If you cannot find beads in the colors to match the hat, you can paint them with plain or pearlized nail varnish. This comes in a vast range of fashion colors and dries quickly to a hard, shiny finish.

MATERIALS
Large beads
Plain or pearlized nail varnish
Hat pin wire with safety guard
Colored feathers
Fine knitting needle or thick wire offcut
Glue gun
Scissors
Modeling clay

1 Thread the beads onto the fine knitting needle, leaving a good space between them. Secure with a small piece of modeling clay. Paint each bead with three coats of colored nail varnish, allowing the varnish to dry between each coat.

2 Using the glue gun, apply a small amount of adhesive to the top end of the hat pin wire.

3 From the other end, thread the beads onto the wire, in the order of your choice, adding more glue if necessary to fix them in place.

4 Trim the feathers to the required length. Apply a thin coat of glue to the end of each one in turn, then carefully push them into the hole in the top bead. Leave to dry.

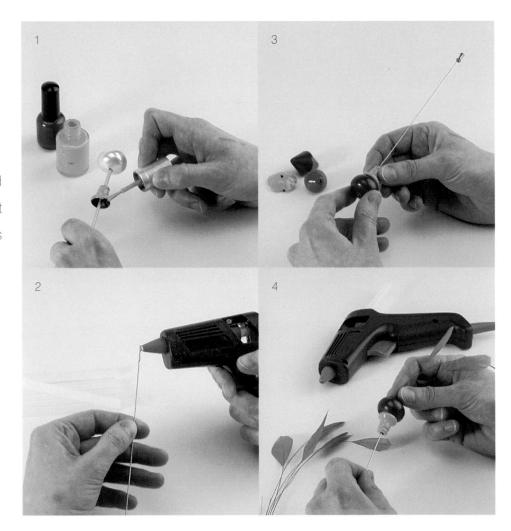

hat pin

bride's bag

Frills of white lace have long been the conventional trimming for bridal wear and accessories. Despite its nostalgic connotations, lace can be used in an unmistakably modern way. This simple bag is just big enough to hold the few essential items that a bride needs on her wedding day: a new powder compact, lipstick, embroidered hand-kerchief, and maybe a good luck charm.

The bag is sewn in sheer cotton with an inset appliqué lace heart motif, and finished off with a discreet lace edging and ribbon roses. The lining is made from soft white lawn, although as an alternative, this could be replaced with colored fabric in a contrasting texture, which will show through the lace and add a hint of pastel shade to the bag.

You could also make similar bags for the bridesmaids in colors to match their dresses, and hide a small gift inside as a token of your thanks.

create your special wedding

Machine-made guipure lace, which has a well-defined pattern, was used for the appliqué. Mount the lawn in a small embroidery frame and back it with tear-off interfacing to support both the lace and the fine fabric while they are being stitched to prevent them from becoming puckered.

MATERIALS

4in./10cm square guipure lace
16 x 22in./40 x 55cm textured cotton
18 x 22in./45 x 55cm white lawn
8in./20cm square tear-off interfacing
Matching sewing cotton
18in./45cm narrow lace trimming
4 ribbon roses
Tracing paper
Pencil
Dressmaker's scissors
Embroidery scissors
Dressmaker's fading pen
6in./15cm diameter embroidery frame
Sewing machine
Sewing kit
Tape measure
Small safety pin
Iron

1 From the textured cotton cut one 11 x 12in./28 x 30cm rectangle (front), one 8 x 10in./ 20 x 25cm rectangle (back), and two 1 x 16in./2.5 x 40cm strips (handles). From the lawn cut two 8 x 10in./20 x 25cm rectangles (lining).

2 Trace the heart template on page 120 and cut it out. Pin to the lace, centering the pattern and draw around it with the dressmaker's fading pen. Trim the lace to ½in./1.5cm from the outline.

3 Tack the lace heart to the center of the front piece and tack the interfacing to the wrong side. Mount the fabric in the embroidery frame.

4 Thread the machine with white sewing thread and set it to a narrow satin stitch. Sew over the outline of the heart. Take the fabric out of the frame and trim the surplus lace close to the stitching.

5 Put the fabric back in the frame and machine stitch a wider satin stitch over the outline to cover the raw edges of the lace.

6 Remove the frame and gently tear away the interfacing. Carefully cut out the cotton fabric from behind the lace using embroidery scissors. Trim the fabric to 8 x 10in./20 x 25cm, ensuring that the heart stays in the center.

7 To make the handles, fold each strip in half lengthwise with right sides facing. Machine stitch ¼in./6mm from the edge.

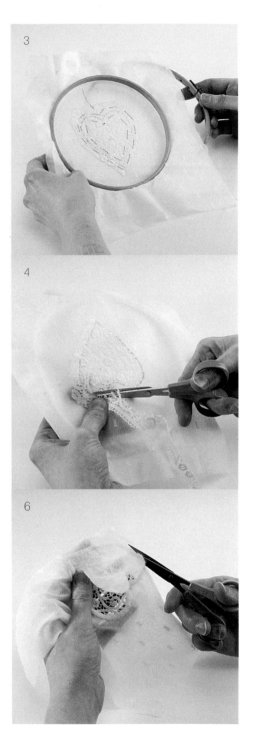

Fix a safety pin to one end and carefully feed it through the fabric tube to turn it right side out.

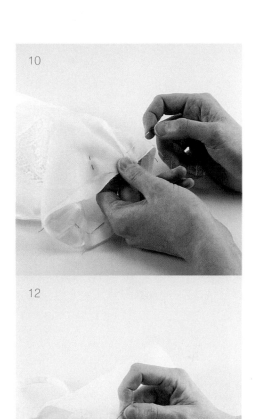

8 Press so that the seam lies along one edge, then top stitch each edge. Trim the handles to 14in./36cm. Tack the ends of one handle to the top edge of the front, and the ends of the other to the top edge of the back, 2in./5cm from the corners.

9 With right sides facing, pin, then tack the front and back pieces together along the side and bottom edges. Machine stitch ½in./1.5cm from the edge, then trim the seam allowance to ¼in./5mm.

10 Join the lining pieces together in the same way, but leave a 3in./8cm gap in the seam along the bottom edge. Turn right side out. Slip the lining inside the bag. Pin and tack the two together around the top of the bag, catching in the ends of the handles, and matching the side seams. Machine stitch, then trim the seam allowance to ¼in./5mm.

11 Turn the bag right side out through the gap. Slip stitch the bottom of the lining and ease it into place inside the bag. Press, then top stitch around the top of the bag ⅛in./3mm from the opening.

12 Slip stitch the narrow lace trimming around the top edge of the bag.

13 As a finishing touch, sew a ribbon rose to the base of each handle.

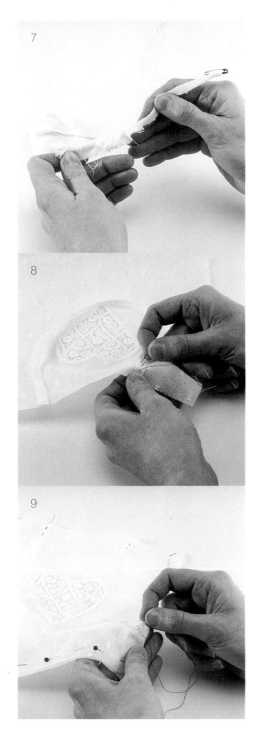

bridesmaid's shoes

Your wedding is a special occasion for everybody involved, not least of whom is the youngest bridesmaid or flower girl, who will no doubt be dreaming of dressing up like a fairy princess for a day. Make her dream come true by completing her outfit with these magical ballet slippers, embroidered with glistening beads in colors to coordinate with her new dress.

Tiny embroidery beads are available from specialist suppliers in a wide range of colors with a matte, translucent, or metallic finish. Choose three or four matching or contrasting shades, depending on the effect you wish to create.

You can easily replace the plain shoelaces in the slippers with narrow ribbon, and it is a good idea to add long, matching ties to make sure that the shoes stay securely on little feet.

Satin ballet shoes in all sizes from toddlers upwards are available from dance suppliers in shades of pink, ivory, and white satin. If necessary, they can be dyed professionally to match the fabric of the bridesmaid's dress.

To work the embroidery, use a fine beading needle or size 11 "sharp" that will pass easily through the beads.

MATERIALS

Satin ballet shoes
1yd/1m of ⅛in./3mm ribbon
⅛in./3mm glass beads in three different colors
1⁄16in./2mm gold glass beads
1yd/1m of ⅓in./8mm satin ribbon
Matching sewing thread
Soft pencil
Fine needle
Embroidery scissors
Sewing kit
Tape measure

1 Cut the narrow ribbon in half. Untie the shoelace and sew one end firmly to an end of one of the ribbons. Pull the other end of the shoelace gently so that the ribbon goes through the ballet shoe and emerges from the opening. Cut off the shoelace and tie the ribbon into a bow.

2 Draw a simple design of curls and spirals around the toe of the shoe with a sharp, soft pencil.

3 Thread the needle with a double length of thread. Stitch the larger beads along the spiral lines, spacing them close together and alternating the colors for each motif.

4 Sew on a sprinkling of small gold beads to fill in the spaces between the spirals.

5 Decorate the second shoe in the same way, reversing the design to make a matching pair.

6 Cut the wide ribbon into four equal lengths. Turning the raw end under, hand stitch two ribbons to each shoe, attaching them to the inside of the seams toward the back of the shoe. Trim the loose ends into fishtails to prevent them from fraying.

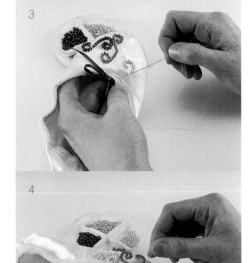

bridal wrap

If you have decided to wear an off-the-shoulder wedding dress or one with short sleeves, this will be a stunning and practical wrap for a cooler wedding day. The gold organza fabric shimmers through the gauzy silk chiffon, and the two layers are caught together with a scattering of silk and velvet petals and pearl beads.

MATERIALS

24in. x 2yd 8in./0.6 x 2m rectangle
cream silk chiffon
24in. x 2yd 8in./0.6 x 2m rectangle
gold metallic organza
Gold sewing thread
Three silk and velvet roses
Small velvet flowers
Selection of pearl beads
Tape measure
Dressmaker's scissors
Embroidery scissors
Sewing machine
Sewing kit

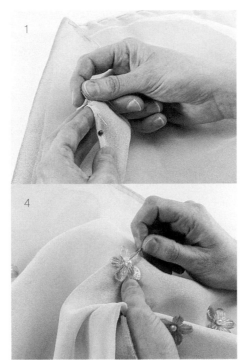

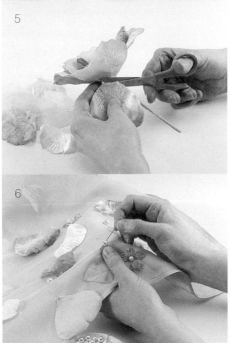

1 With right sides together, pin and tack the two pieces of fabric together around the outside edge.

2 Thread the sewing machine with the gold thread and stitch ½in./1.5cm from the edge. Leave a 6in./15cm gap at the center of one long side. Trim the seam allowance to ¼in./6mm, then turn the wrap the right way out through the gap.

3 Tack the sides of the gap together, then work two closely spaced rounds of top stitch in gold thread around the outside edge of the wrap.

4 Sew half the velvet flowers across the bottom 20in./50cm of both ends of the wrap, spacing them evenly. Sew a small pearl bead in the center of each one.

5 Carefully snip the petals from the roses. Sew half of them across each end of the wrap in the spaces between the flowers. Catch down the pointed end of the petals with a few hand stitches worked in gold thread.

6 Finish off by sewing the remaining pearls in the spaces between the petals and the flowers.

ring pocket

The precious wedding rings exchanged by the bride and groom play a key role in every marriage ceremony, and symbolize the devotion of the newly married couple. Before you entrust them to the ring bearer, make sure that they will be kept safely together in this sumptuous drawstring pocket.

It is made from cotton velvet in two contrasting colors—the bag is in a rich shade of purple and the lining is a vibrant tangerine—but you could substitute cream or white for a more muted look. Scraps of fabric or lace left over from the wedding dress and lined with satin would also make a very special pocket.

The small silver bells that decorate the ends of the cord come from India, where they are used to embellish embroidered garments and accessories, but if you cannot find anything similar, two or three lucky charms—a clover leaf, a heart, and a horseshoe—would make a whimsical substitute.

The drawstrings are made from crocheted embroidery thread in a rich orange to match the lining, but if you prefer, you could simply make two plaited lengths. Fine silk cord or narrow velvet ribbon would also make good alternative ties.

MATERIALS

5 x 10in./12 x 25cm orange velvet
5 x 10in./12 x 25cm purple velvet
Matching sewing thread
Skein of orange embroidery thread
6 small silver bells
Pencil
Ruler
Tracing paper
Sewing machine
Sewing kit
Tape measure
Dressmaker's scissors
Dressmaker's pins
Chalk pencil
1.75 crochet hook
Small safety pin

1 Trace the template on page 120 and use it to cut out one orange velvet rectangle and one purple velvet rectangle. Cut eight small notches along the sides of the purple velvet as indicated on the template.

2 Fold the orange velvet rectangle in half lengthwise with right sides together. Pin and tack the two side edges together, then machine stitch ½in./1.5cm from the edge. Clip the corners.

3 Pin and tack the purple velvet rectangle in the same way, lining up the notches. Machine stitch as before but leave a gap in the stitching between the notches on each side.

4 Tack a ½in./1.5cm turning to the wrong side around the top of both bags, opening out the side seams so that they lie flat.

5 Turn the purple bag right side out. Slip the orange lining inside the bag and line it up so that the seams match. Pin and tack together around the top edge so that ⅛in./3mm of the orange lining peeps above the top of the purple bag.

6 Slip stitch the two pieces together, sewing through the top layer of orange velvet only.

7 Mark the drawstring channel onto the purple velvet by lightly ruling a chalk pencil line at each end of the gaps in the side seams at front and back.

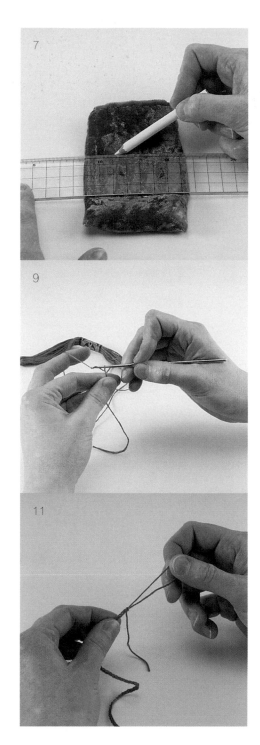

8 Work a line of small running stitch through the bag and the lining over each line on both sides.

9 To start the drawstring cord, make a slip knot at the end of the embroidery thread and insert the hook into the loop. Take the thread over the hook.

10 Draw the thread through the loop to make the first chain stitch, then continue making chain stitches until the cord measures 10in./25cm.

11 To finish off, slip the hook out of the loop and cut the thread to leave a 2in./5cm tail. Pull the loose end through the loop and pull tightly.

12 Make a second drawstring cord in the same way.

13 Attach a small safety pin to the end of one of the cords. Insert it through one opening in the drawstring channel and thread it through both sides of the bag.

14 Thread the second cord through the other opening and around the bag in the same way.

15 Thread three bells onto the end of each chain and stitch in place. Neaten the ends of the cord.

16 Slip the two rings inside the bag and pull up the drawstrings securely to close the top and keep them safe.

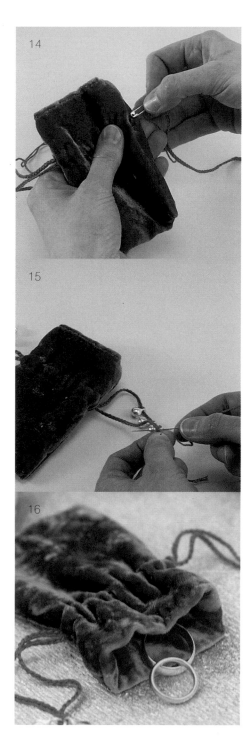

reception

The wedding breakfast—the first meal shared by the bride and groom as man and wife—was traditionally a time of great festivity. Today's equivalent is the reception and, after the long weeks of anticipation and organization, this is the time when you can both relax and begin to celebrate in earnest after the nervous excitement of the marriage ceremony. You will have the chance to meet members of your extended family, catch up with old acquaintances, and chat with close friends and relatives.

This is the one party you will want to remember forever, so make it special with your own personal touches—keepsake favors, handwritten menu cards, and place markers. Decorate the reception room with swags and garlands of flowers, and make a special centerpiece for each table. You can add to the romantic ambience of an evening event with the soft flames from candles studded with glittering sequins.

The venue can be anywhere from a marquee in the garden to a function room at your favorite local restaurant or hotel. Your choice of meal and entertainment will depend upon the number of people you have invited and the timing of the service, as well as the location. It can be anything from a simple lunch, buffet, or early supper, to a grand dinner followed by a dance. Whatever the scale, spend time selecting a suitable menu, bearing in mind that you will probably have to cater for a range of ages and tastes. Provide a seating plan at the entrance to the room, along with individual name cards at each place setting, or ensure that there are plenty of tables and chairs for a more casual buffet.

As your guests arrive, a receiving line gives the two of you and your respective parents the chance to greet everyone personally and to be introduced to anybody you have not met previously. This custom has its origins in the folk belief that a couple is specially blessed on the day of their marriage and can impart good fortune simply by shaking hands.

Even a low-key wedding will feature a champagne toast, the ceremonial cutting of the cake, and at least one speech. You can guarantee that you will have your own unique record of these events by equipping each table with a single-use flash camera and asking your guests to take their own candid snaps during the course of the party.

Delicate skeleton leaves, gauzy ribbon, and transparent tracing paper have been combined to make these pretty cards, which extend the theme of flowers and foliage to other aspects of the table setting. The menu itself can be handwritten with a gold or silver pen, or printed on a separate slip sheet and glued inside the folded card.

MATERIALS

Colored heavy tracing paper
Skeleton leaves
⅓in./8mm wide gauzy ribbon
Sharp pencil
Metal ruler
Cutting board
Craft knife
Eraser
Craft scissors
Glue stick

1 Cut an 8in./20cm square from the tracing paper. Mark the midpoints of two opposite sides and rule a pencil line between them. On the cutting mat, gently score along the line using the metal ruler and craft knife. Rub out the pencil marks.

2 Carefully fold the paper in half along the scored line. Give definition to the shape by smoothing along the crease with the handle of the scissors.

3 Fold a 12in./30cm length of gauzy ribbon in half and knot it around the bottom of the leaf stalk. Tie the ends in a bow.

4 Attach the leaf to the center front of the card using a sparing amount of glue and smooth it in place.

5 Trim the ends of the ribbon and glue them down to the card.

menu card

napkin ring

A simple sprig of dark green ivy, bound with sparkling glass beads and gauzy ribbon, provides an unusual natural alternative to the conventional napkin ring. Depending on the season, you could also use decorative grasses, cuttings of fragrant honeysuckle, jasmine, or autumnal red Virginia creeper, to tie in with the flower arrangements. These decorations should be made as close to the time of the reception as possible to ensure that the flowers or foliage are fresh.

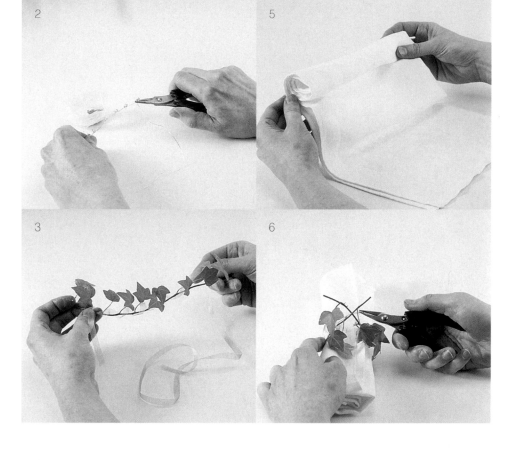

MATERIALS

6in./15cm lengths of small-leaved ivy
Rocaille beads
Rose wire
⅓in./1cm wide ribbon
Small colored glass beads
Linen napkins
Wire cutters
Flat-nosed pliers
Ruler

1 Cut a 10in./25cm length of rose wire. Thread on three beads and slide them to 1½in./4cm from the end. Twist the beads with the flat-nosed pliers to keep them in place on the wire.

2 Thread more groups of beads at approximately ⅔in./2cm intervals to within 1½in./4cm from the other end.

3 Wrap a length of ribbon loosely around the ivy, leaving a 3in./8cm length at each end.

4 Twist the beaded wire around the ivy stem and the ribbon.

5 Fold a napkin in half and roll it up.

6 Wrap the decorated ivy round the center of the napkin. Twist the ends of the wire together. Flatten the ends with the pliers. Loosely knot the ends of the ribbon.

7 If necessary, store the napkins in a cool place overnight, insuring that the leaves do not become crushed.

Inject a little color at each table setting by planting up miniature flower pots to identify your guests' seating places. Write the name of each guest on a small card and attach it to a heart-shaped marker twisted from garden wire.

The silver paint used on the flower pot contrasts beautifully with the pale blue petals of the miniature campanula, but you may wish to use another color to match the flowers in your other arrangements. Aerosol craft paint is quick and easy to use, and gives an even coverage on the plain terra-cotta pot.

MATERIALS
Galvanized garden wire
Mount board
2in./5cm flower pots
Small trailing plant
Gravel
Pliers
Knitting needle
Black pen and ruler
Spray craft paint

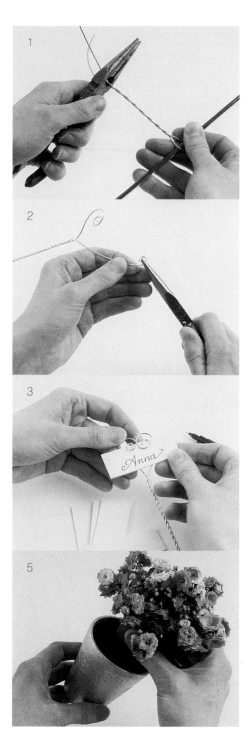

1 For the marker, cut a 16in./40cm length of garden wire. Bend it in half and hold the top 2in./5cm firmly with the flat part of the pliers. Insert the knitting needle into the loop and twist it clockwise to make the stem.

2 Using the pliers, twist each short end into a spiral to make a heart shape.

3 Cut a 1 x 2¾in./2.5 x 7cm rectangle of mount board. Write a guest's name on it, and slip the card under the wire spirals.

4 Spray the flower pot with silver paint and allow to dry.

5 Sprinkle a thin layer of gravel at the bottom of the pot and place the plant inside.

6 Fix the name marker toward the front of the pot.

Anna

place
setting

monogrammed glasses

The champagne toast gives the assembled guests their first opportunity to join together in celebration and drink to the future happiness of the bride and groom. Make it extra special with these elegant champagne flutes, decorated with the first initials of your names.

Stenciling is a straightforward technique, but to transfer a detailed image, such as these flowing letters, onto a curved surface you will need to use an adhesive stencil. The removable adhesive film made for airbrush work is easy to use and gives a sharp outline.

MATERIALS

Tall plain champagne glasses
Tracing paper
Lo-tack clear adhesive film
White matte glass paint
Black marker pen
Craft scissors
Small curved-blade scissors
Soft cloth
High density sponge

1 Use an alphabet from a copyright-free sourcebook and enlarge it to the size required. Trace off the outline of the two letters and an ampersand. Remember to make "bridges" to link the two sides of open letters such as "O" or "B."

2 Cut a piece of adhesive film slightly larger than the monogram and peel off the backing. Fix it to the right side of the tracing paper.

3 Cut out the letters with the curved-blade scissors to give a smooth line.

4 Carefully peel the two layers apart and attach the stencil to the surface of a clean glass. Rub it down with a soft cloth to remove any air bubbles.

5 Dab a thin layer of white glass paint over the stencil with a small piece of sponge. Allow to dry, then apply a second coat.

6 Leave for several hours to dry completely, then carefully remove the stencil. Follow the manufacturer's instructions to set the paint and for the aftercare of the glass.

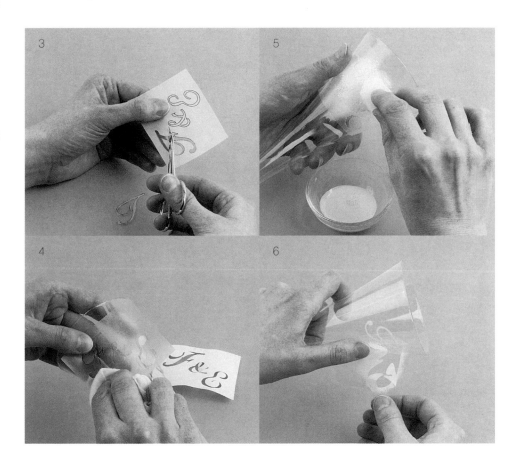

table runner

Use rubber craft stamps to create an embossed design of hearts and flowers across the surface of a velvet tablecloth. The pressing technique is easy to pick up, but it is worth practicing first on a scrap of fabric. Ensure that the stamps you choose are not made from polymer plastic, as this will melt under the heat of the iron.

MATERIALS

Dressmaking velvet
Matching sewing thread
Two rubber stamps
Sewing kit
Sewing machine
Tape measure
Iron

1 Cut out a square or rectangle of velvet to the required size, adding on an extra 1in./3cm all round. Turn under and tack a ½in./1.5cm double hem along each side.

2 Thread the sewing machine with matching sewing thread, then sew a round of straight stitch ¼in./6mm from the fold. Work a second round of stitches ⅛in./ 3mm further in.

3 Adjust the iron to the hottest setting and allow to warm up.

4 Place a stamp face up on a heat resistant work surface, then lay the velvet right side down over it. Press the iron onto the wrong side of the fabric for thirty seconds without moving. If you are using a steam iron, avoid the part of the sole where the holes are, as these will not leave an impression on the stamp.

5 Repeat this process over the whole surface of the velvet, alternating the two stamps and placing them at different angles to create a varied pattern.

favors

According to the English dictionary, a favor is "a small gift or toy given to a guest at a party" or "a token of love, goodwill..." Small, frivolous presents are usually offered by the bride and groom to their guests.

Spring brides in the eighteenth century tied up sprigs of orange blossom with lengths of silver lace and satin ribbon and handed them out to their friends and relatives. According to the Language of Flowers, this symbolized "bridal festivity." The usual present given today is a bonbonière—a bundle of sugared almonds wrapped in circles of net or organza. These represent fertility, and so are eaten as a wish for a fruitful marriage.

A more original idea is to make these exuberant confections from lollipops dressed up in bright translucent paper and decked with ribbons. Anybody who can resist the temptation to unwrap and eat them right away can take them home as a souvenir of the happy day.

Allow yourselves the fun of returning to childhood tastes when buying the materials for this project. Hunt around confectioners for the most colorful lollipops and try to find the smallest, brightest stickers to decorate the wrapping. The bows are made from narrow satin ribbon, but curls of glittering paper gift ribbon would look equally attractive.

MATERIALS
Assorted lollipops
Translucent wrapping paper
in a range of colors
Narrow ribbon in a range of colors
Small stickers in a range of
shapes and sizes
Craft scissors
Ruler

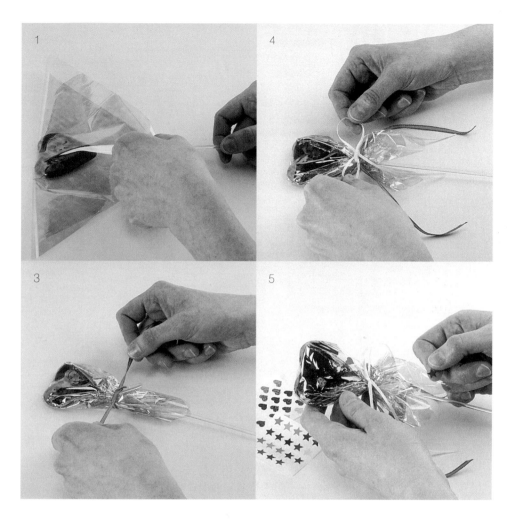

1 Cut a 8in./20cm square of translucent paper. Remove any existing wrapping from the lollipop and place the stick diagonally across one corner of the paper so that the head lies in the center of the square. Bring the upper corner down over the lollipop.

2 Fold the two side corners of the paper downward and inward to cover the head of the lollipop.

3 Cut a 10in./25cm length of narrow ribbon and knot it around the paper just below the head of the lollipop. Tie the ends into a bow.

4 Cut a 10in./25cm length of ribbon in a different color, knot it over the first and make another bow.

5 As a finishing touch, add a few small stickers to the wrapping.

A lighted candle represents hope and the continuity of life, making it a fitting symbol for a wedding reception. This simple, rectangular candle has been embellished with silver beads and reflective metal sequins to create a shimmering focal point on the table at an evening reception. Make a smaller version to accompany each place setting so that the flickering light of the flames creates a warm and intimate atmosphere for your guests.

Use short pins (available from good craft suppliers) rather than long dressmaker's pins to fix the sequins to the candle. You may find that it helps to wear a thimble when pushing the pins into the wax. Remember that lighted candles should never be left unattended, and keep them well out of the reach of children.

1 Cut two pieces of paper the same shape and size as the long and short sides of the candle. Draw two diagonal lines across each one to mark the center point. Lay the sequins out on the paper in a symmetrical pattern, taking time to achieve a pleasing arrangement.

2 Measure the centerpoint of the long side of the candle and mark it with a pinprick. Thread a pearl bead onto a pin and then the sequin from the center of the design, and pin carefully into the middle of the candle.

3 Pin the next ring of sequins around the center.

4 Pin the other sequins in place to complete the design, first threading a small round or molded silver bead or a pearl onto the pin.

5 Decorate the opposite side and the ends of the candle in the same way.

studded candle

setting up home

The days when married life started with the groom ceremoniously carrying his bride over the threshold of their new home may seem to belong to the past, but the hope, expectation, and optimism with which all newly married couples embark on their shared life are unchanging.

The celebration and goodwill that accompanies the wedding ceremony will be captured in the many photographs of you and your guests, and summed up in the letters, cards, and gifts you receive during the preceding weeks. Capture these memories, which will become more treasured over the years, by making the wallet on page 109 to preserve the ephemera, and the portfolio on page 112 to store your pictures.

Whether or not you have moved into a new house or apartment, you are bound to have been given an extensive selection of presents with which to furnish and equip your home. Many couples opt for a gift registry at their favorite department store. The wedding list, however, is a comparatively recent innovation. The formal etiquette of earlier generations dictated that it was not correct behavior to ask for specific items. Wedding presents had to be essentially decorative, not practical, and the choice had to be left to the discretion of the guests, while the bride herself provided the majority of everyday items, essential for setting up her new home.

In the nineteenth century, a girl would have been expected to spend her teenage years preparing her hope chest to take with her when she married. Her *trousseau*, which translates literally as "little bundle," was made up of household linen, hand-embroidered bed clothes, towels, quilts, pillow shams, and her own personal lingerie and night clothes. Although today the bride typically receives similar items as gifts or as part of her bridal shower, it is fun and rewarding to stitch a small quilt or throw just for yourself and your husband, to symbolize your new life together.

Your front door key is an essentially utilitarian object, but historically a key was given and accepted as a sign of true love—locking or unlocking the door of the heart—so you could make the key fob on page 117 as a tangible expression of your shared affection. Likewise, the family tree on page 106 can be made to display photographs of your extended family, with room for any new additions!

patchwork quilt

Many families have acquired a collection of antique table linen, napkins, tray cloths, and embroidered mats through the years. These are often stored away, unused, and passed from one generation to the next, but with this project you can give them a new lease on life and create your own family heirloom. Ask friends and relations from both sides of the family and collect a very personal assortment of white fabrics to make this classic patchwork quilt for your new home.

Despite its appearance, only the most basic sewing techniques are used to create the quilt, making it an ideal project for a beginner. Don't worry too much if the corners don't quite join up perfectly, the pearl buttons will disguise any inaccuracies in the seaming. A sewing machine is used throughout, but you may prefer to work the quilting by hand.

MATERIALS

Old linen, damask, embroidered mats,
and lace fabrics

White sewing thread

1yd 14in./1.27m polyester or
cotton batting

1yd 14in./1.27m cotton sheeting
for the backing

Four 8in. x 1yd 8in./0.2 x 1.35m strips
striped white fabric for the border

83 pearl shirt buttons

Sewing kit

Sewing machine

Dressmaker's scissors

Chalk pencil

Protractor

Iron

Finished size is approximately
1yd 14in./1m 27cm square

1 For the patchwork pieces, cut 110 5in./12.5cm squares from the white fabrics, avoiding any worn or damaged areas. Cut 13 of these in half diagonally to make 26 triangles and cut two of these triangles in half to make 4 smaller triangles that will fit into the corners.

2 Start by laying out all the patches in a large square. Place the first seven patches in a row "on point" (like diamonds), then fit the next row of six patches in the spaces in between them. Continue adding alternate rows of seven, then six patches.

3 Finish off the square by placing the large triangles along the edges and the

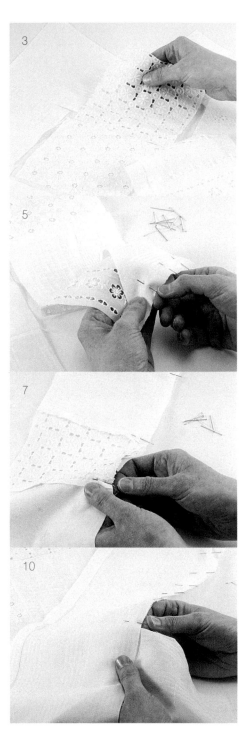

small triangles at the corners. Swap the patches around until you are satisfied with the arrangement of patterns and textures.

4 Join the patches together in diagonal strips, starting at one corner. Pin and tack the long side of the small triangle to the first square. Machine stitch together, leaving a seam allowance of ¼in./6mm. Press the seam open.

5 Sew the long sides of the two large triangles to each side of the first square and press. Stitch the next three squares together, add a triangle to each end and press. Join the rest of the patches in this way.

6 Starting again at the corner, pin and tack the first two strips together, matching the seams. Machine stitch ¼in./6mm from the edge and press the seam open.

7 Continue joining the strips in this way as far as the center, then start again at the opposite corner. Machine stitch the two triangles together.

8 Press under a ½in./1.5cm turning along one long edge of each border strip and mark the midpoint of the other (raw) edge with a chalk pencil.

9 Match the midpoint of the first border strip to the center of one side of the patchwork square, then pin and tack together with right sides facing. The ends of the border will overlap the square at

each end. Machine stitch, leaving a seam allowance of ½in./1.5cm.

10 Sew on the remaining three strips in the same way and press all the seam allowances toward the border.

11 The corners are mitred by hand. Fold the end of one strip under at a forty-five degree angle (use a protractor to ensure it is accurate) and press. Pin the fold flat onto the adjoining overlap and tack in place. Slip stitch along the join, then trim the surplus fabric leaving a ½in./1.5cm seam allowance.

12 Lay the patchwork face down, then place the batting centrally over it, leaving an equal margin all round. Put the backing over the batting then baste all three layers together, smoothing constantly to ensure they lie flat. Work long lines of tacking stitch, starting from the center outwards.

13 To quilt the throw, machine or hand stitch along each seam, then sew around the outside edge of the square.

14 Turn the border edges to the back of the quilt to conceal the raw edges of the batting and backing. Pin, then tack in place, folding the corners at right angles. Slip stitch the folded edges of the border to the backing.

15 Finish off the throw by sewing a pearl button to each point where the patchwork squares meet.

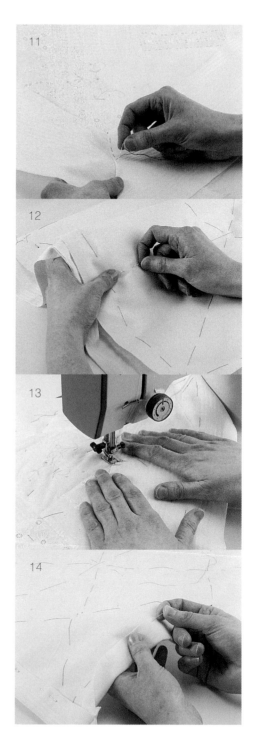

family tree

Family trees are not just for those with an interest in genealogy. Make this Mexican-style wire work version to symbolize the joining together of your two families and decorate the branches with scaled-down treasured snapshots of relations and mutual friends. To preserve your precious originals, reshoot photographs on black-and-white film, or reduce the images with a computer scanner or photocopier.

MATERIALS

2.0 gauge galvanized wire
1.0 gauge galvanized wire
Fine brass wire
Craft foil
Selection of small photographs
Round-nosed pliers
Flat-nosed pliers
Wire cutters
Blunt pencil
Old scissors
Glue gun

1 Enlarge the template on page 121 on a photocopier to the size indicated.

2 Cut a piece of 2.0 gauge galvanized wire to fit along each of the curved lines. Use the round-nosed pliers to bend the wire into spirals, taking care to keep the sharp ends away from your hands.

3 Bind the wires together where indicated on the template using lengths of fine brass wire. Twist the ends together on the wrong side with the flat-nosed pliers and clip to ¼in./6mm with the wire cutters. Squeeze the ends flat against the coiled wire using the flat-nosed pliers.

4 Make the tree up in two halves, then bind the pieces together to make a trunk using 1.0 gauge galvanized wire. Finish off the ends securely as before.

5 Using the picture opposite as a guide, draw a series of leaves in different sizes onto the shiny side of the craft foil, with the blunt pencil. Press gently to create a ridged outline.

6 Cut out each leaf around the outline with a pair of old scissors.

7 Stick the leaves onto the branches using the glue gun.

8 Cut the photographs down to 1 x 2in./2.5 x 5cm. Glue them onto the branches in the spaces between the leaves.

memento wallet

Keep all the favorite memories of your special day safely together in this concertina wallet, which is certain to become a family keepsake.

The classic white linen covers open up to reveal a concertina of individual paper envelopes in which to store the various items of ephemera that you will collect during the run up to the date and on the wedding day itself —a menu, an invitation, photographs, a letter or secret message, pressed flowers, and even the ribbon from the bridal bouquet.

The folding wallet is deceptively straightforward to make. Practice machine stitching on a scrap of paper before starting to sew the inner section to ensure that the tension is correct. Set the stitch length to maximum; if the perforations are too close together the paper will split.

MATERIALS
16½ x 23½in./42 x 60cm sheet
of watercolor paper
Two 6½in./16cm squares
of mount board
Three 8¾in./22cm squares
of white linen
Pearl button
White sewing thread
White crochet thread
Metal ruler
Sharp pencil and eraser
Craft knife
Cutting mat
Craft scissors
Set square
Removable tape
Sewing machine
PVA adhesive
Glue brush
Double-sided tape
Iron

1 Draw the inner section of the wallet by transferring the measurements on the template on page 122 onto the watercolor paper. Lightly mark the stitch line with the sharp pencil.

2 Cut out along the outline. Score lightly over the two fold lines with the craft knife and metal ruler on the cutting mat.

3 Fold the lower edge upward along the scored lines and secure in place with removable tape.

4 Thread the sewing machine with white thread and set the stitch length to ⅛in./4mm.

5 With the folded side of the paper facing downward and the flaps facing down, start stitching at the top right corner. Leaving a margin of ⅛in/4mm, join the two outer edges and stitch around the flap. Sew down the first dividing line, then back up along the second.

6 Stitch around the remaining flaps and dividing lines in the same way. Fold the flaps downward along the scored line.

7 To make the front and back covers, coat one side of a mount board square with a thin layer of PVA. Position it, glue side down, in the center of one linen square. Glue the surplus fabric down on the wrong side, mitring the corners.

8 Cut the remaining linen square in half diagonally. Press under a narrow hem along each short edge with an iron, then tack in place. Machine stitch down with two lines of stitches.

9 Fix a length of double-sided tape along the top back edge of one cover. Peel off the backing. Mark the center front with a pin. Line the point of the triangle up with the pin and fold the surplus fabric to the back. Press it firmly onto the tape and trim neatly.

10 Make each tassel by winding the white sewing thread approximately 300 times around a 3in./7cm wide scrap of card. Thread a length of crochet cotton under the strands and knot tightly.

11 Slip the loop off the card and bind the neck of the tassel with sewing cotton. Sew in the end of the thread, then cut through the loop and trim the tassel.

12 Stitch the tassels to the wrong side of the triangle point, then sew the button to the right side.

13 Attach the front and back panels to the folded inner section with strips of double-sided tape.

14 To protect the linen cover from wear and tear, you could store the wallet in a shallow box lined with tissue paper.

photograph portfolio

The official pictures, taken by a professional photographer, will provide lifelong memories of your wedding day, and they should be displayed accordingly. This paper-covered folder makes a perfect substitute for the more conventional presentation album. Its design is inspired by an artist's portfolio, and the pictures are mounted on individual sheets with old-fashioned corner mounts. There is also room to store the more informal (and often more revealing) snapshots taken by your guests before and after the ceremony or at the reception, along with the photographs from your honeymoon.

The cardboard covers are backed with a geometric print and tied with tape, but for a more luxurious feel, you may wish to use a marble-effect paper and velvet or satin ribbons. To protect the surface of the photographs, cut sheets of tissue or tracing paper to place between the leaves.

MATERIALS

Two 8¼ x 11¾in./21 x 30cm (A4) rectangles of thick card
Two 11¾ x 16½in./30 x 42cm (A3) rectangles of patterned paper
2yd/2m of ¾in./1.8cm wide cotton tape
Parchment-effect card
Dark gray card
Tissue paper
Spray mount
Craft scissors
Metal ruler
Craft knife
Cutting mat
Double-sided tape
Sharp pencil
Eraser

1 Spray the wrong side of one of the paper rectangles lightly with spray mount and place a rectangle of thick cardboard in the center. Cut off the corners and fold the flaps to the back of the card. Smooth them into place. Make the second cover board in the same way.

2 Mark a ¹⁄₁₆ x ⅝in./2 x 18mm slot in the center of each short side and one long side of both cover boards. Cut them out on the cutting mat with the metal ruler and craft knife.

3 Cut the tape into six 12in./33cm lengths. Thread one piece through each slot and stick the end down on the wrong side with a short piece of double-sided tape.

4 Trim the ends of the tapes into fish tails to prevent them fraying.

5 From the parchment-effect card, cut an 11½ x 17in./29 x 43cm rectangle to make the lining. With a sharp pencil draw two points on each long side 8¼in./21cm in from the corners. These points mark the spine fold.

6 Place the card on the cutting mat. Score across the width of the card to join the two sets of marks with the ruler and craft knife, then erase the pencil marks.

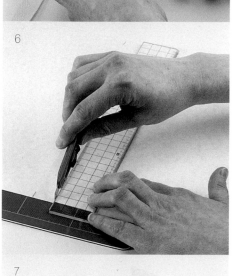

7 Cut out one large flap and two small flaps from the parchment-effect card, using the templates on pages 123 and 124 as guides. Score lightly where indicated by the dotted lines, then fold along the scores.

8 Attach lengths of double-sided tape to the straight edge of the flaps, where indicated on the templates, then stick them to the wrong side of the lining.

9 Use more double-sided tape to fix the cover boards to the wrong side of the lining. Line up the two edges without ties along the spine folds and leave an equal margin around the top and side edges.

10 Fold carefully into shape along the spine.

11 Cut 8 x 11in./20 x 28cm sheets of dark gray card to go inside the portfolio, tearing the edges against a ruler to create a deckle finish.

12 Mount your photographs on the card sheets. Place them carefully inside the portfolio with a sheet of tissue paper (cut to size) between each one to protect the surface of the photographs. Close the portfolio by tying the three pairs of tapes into decorative knots or bows.

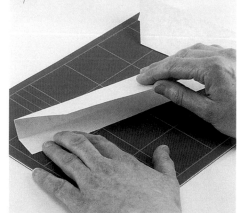

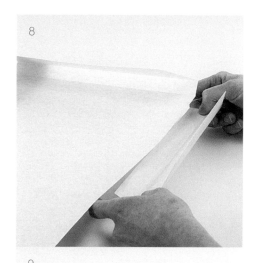

You will always by able to find
the spare set of keys to your
home when they are securely
fixed to this oversized key fob.
It features the charming
"Little House" design—a
traditional American patchwork
motif, which has been adapted
for appliqué.

MATERIALS

6 x 10in./15 x 25cm piece of white linen
Scraps of brightly colored cotton fabric
6 x 10in./15 x 25cm cotton batting
20 x 1½in./50 x 4cm strip
of striped fabric
Matching sewing threads
Tracing paper, sharp pencil, and ruler
Sewing kit
Iron
Embroidery scissors

1 Trace and cut out the appliqué shapes
on page 124: front wall, side wall, roof,
two chimneys, two windows, and a door.
From the fabric scraps, cut a piece to
cover each paper shape, adding a ¼in./
6mm turning all round.

2 Trace and cut out the main shape of the
key fob from the template on page 124
and use it to cut two pieces of white linen
and two pieces of batting.

3 Tack the fabric to the wrong side of the
paper appliqué shapes, turning over a
narrow margin all round and mitring the
corners neatly.

4 Press each appliqué shape from the
wrong side to set the folds, then remove
the tacking and the papers.

5 Tack the two walls and the roof to one
of the main linen pieces, using the
template as a guide to position them. Slip
stitch down around the outside edge with
matching sewing thread.

6 Tack and slip stitch the door, windows,
and chimneys.

7 Sandwich the two batting pieces
between the two plain pieces of linen, so
that the appliqué is facing upward. Pin the
four layers together, then tack around the
outside edge.

8 To make the binding, press the strip of
striped fabric in half lengthwise, then fold
and press each edge to the center.

9 Starting at the point, and mitring the
corners as you work, fold the binding over
the raw edges of the key fob. Pin and tack
in place, cutting off the surplus. Slip stitch
the folded edge to the linen on both front
and back using matching thread. Remove
the tacking thread.

10 Use the remaining binding to make a
small loop to fix the keys to the fob.

create your special wedding

key fob

templates

organizer file

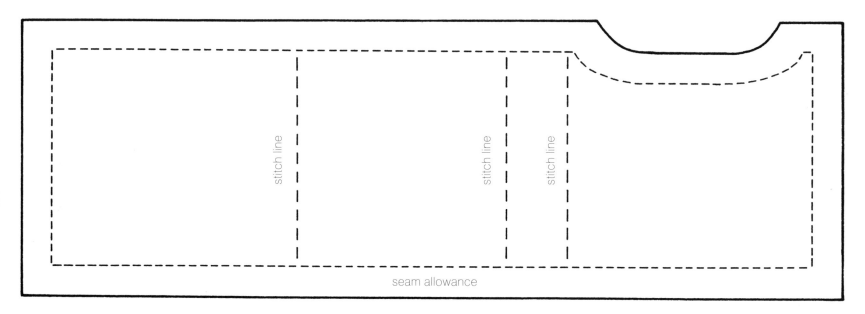

stitch line

stitch line

stitch line

seam allowance

Enlarge to 11in./28cm.

confetti box

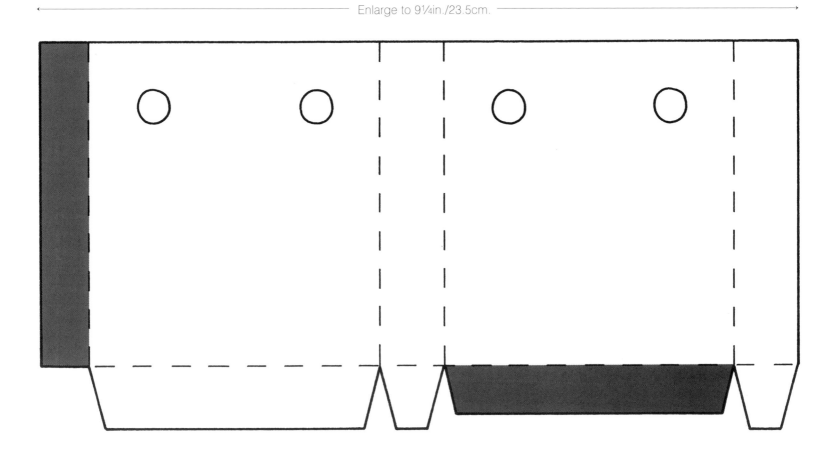

bride's bag

actual size

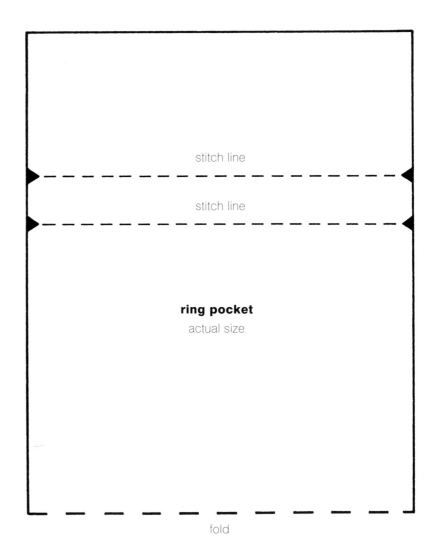

stitch line

stitch line

ring pocket

actual size

fold

family tree

memento wallet

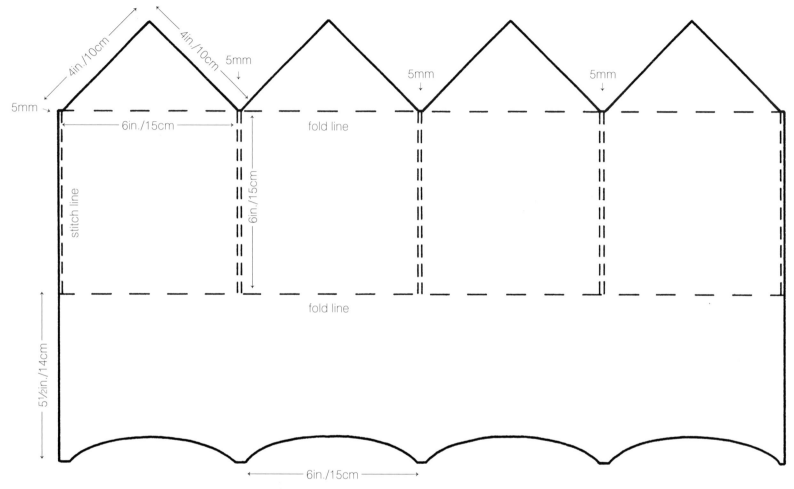

5mm

4in./10cm 4in./10cm 5mm

5mm 5mm

5mm

fold line

6in./15cm

6in./15cm

stitch line

fold line

5½in./14cm

6in./15cm

**photograph portfolio
large flap**

Enlarge to 11½in./29cm.

templates

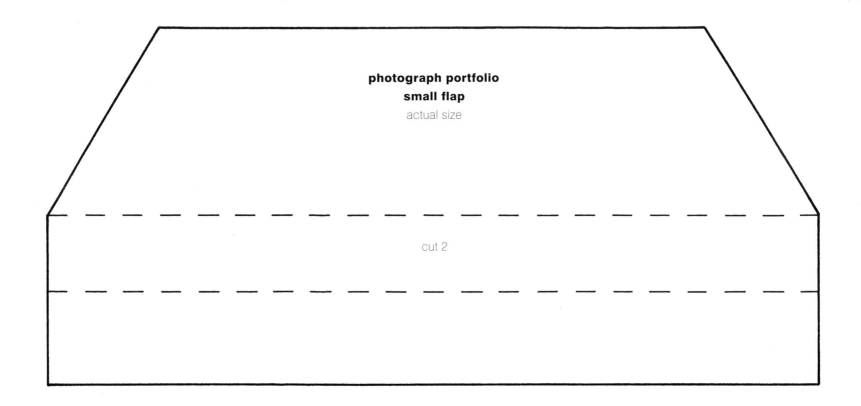

photograph portfolio
small flap
actual size

cut 2

key fob
actual size

create your special wedding

credits

The publishers would like to thank the following companies for their help with the photography of this book.

Thorns Furniture & Catering Hire, 62 Garman Road, Tottenham, London N17 0UT, tel: 020 8801 4444, for the trestle table, gilt chairs, and lilac damask linen.

Presentation Hire, Glendower Road, Leominster, Herefordshire HR6 0RL, tel: 01568 616638, for the white and wine-colored damask table linen.

Rachel Skinner Millinery, 13 Princess Road, London NW1 8JR, tel: 020 7209 0066, for the fuchsia hat and ivory tulle feather piece for the hat pin project.

Cologne & Cotton, 791 Fulham Road, London SW6 5HD, tel: 020 7736 9261, for toiletries and handkerchiefs.

Mark Maynard Antiques, 652 Fulham Road, London SW6 5PU, tel: 020 7731 3533, for the French-style chair, dressing table, and gilt dressing mirror.

The Conran Shop, Michelin House, 81 Fulham Road, London SW3 6RD, tel: 020 7589 7401, for the champagne flutes, white crockery with gold bands, cutlery, tinted colored coffee cups and saucers, and stationery accessories.

Emma Hope Shoes, 53 Sloane Square, London SW1X 8AX, tel: 020 7259 9566, for the ivory wedding shoes.

Joyce Jackson Veils, for stockists information call 01745 343 6891, for the pearl detail fine net veil.

index

create your special wedding